THE
BOOK OF
REVELATION

A STUDY GUIDE

DAVID MEEKS
AND
MICHAEL FILIPEK

LetUsReason
PUBLISHING

LetUsReason Publishing, Springfield, NJ
ISBN 979-8-9871064-2-6 (Paperback)
ISBN 979-8-9871064-3-3 (eBook)

Cover design by Jeffrey Mardis and Michael Filipek.

Cover art: *The Second Coming* by Jon McNaughton.

CONTENTS

1

OVERVIEW OF REVELATION

Introduction

The book of Revelation is the last book in the Bible and the consummation of all revealed truth. It is the Revelation of Jesus Christ, unveiling future events while confirming His true identity and ultimate victory. It reassures the Church that Jesus was, is, and will always be in control. It also promises us that He is coming back soon, warning us to watch and remain ready.

Although many Christians are intimidated by the rich symbolism used in Revelation, we should recognize that God's intention was for us to understand the important truths expressed within this book. The book's very name comes from the Greek word *apokalypsis*, which means "to reveal or to unveil; to open to understanding what otherwise could not be comprehended." Through diligent study, we absolutely can discern the content of Revelation.

Since the book of Revelation describes a vision, its contents are often revealed symbolically. However, Revelation self-defines much of its own symbolism. And in the instances where it does not, many other passages in scripture can help us understand their meaning.

We must keep in mind that the author was describing futuristic events that often defied description. Many of these concepts would have been inexplicable to his own first-century understanding and vocabulary. Therefore, he often incorporates the use of similes (using "like" or "as" to draw comparisons) to express what he was seeing. Imagine the great difficulty a person living in the 1800s would have in attempting to describe a vision of modern times. The author of Revelation was attempting to describe events that would take place over two thousand years into the future!

Prior to its writing, much of Revelation's futuristic content had already been prophetically disclosed elsewhere in scripture. In fact, of Revelation's 404 verses, at least 265 of them refer or allude to approximately 550 Old Testament verses. It contains numerous references to symbolism used in other prophecies and visions, such as the Old Testament visions of Daniel, Ezekiel, and Zechariah. However, Revelation provides sharper detail and supplies additional information that better informs our understanding of how these prophecies will come to pass within a chronological sequence. We can say that Revelation acts as the framework for organizing the Bible's many prophecies that relate to the end-times.

How Can We Understand Revelation?

- One key to sound Bible interpretation (especially concerning the book of Revelation) is to maintain a **consistent hermeneutic.**
- Hermeneutics is the theory and methodology of the interpretation of texts – in this case, the Bible.
- A **literal** hermeneutic (or normal method of interpreting scripture) means that unless the verse or

passage clearly indicates that the author was using figurative language, **it should be understood in its normal, plain, literal, contextual, and historical sense.** If the plain meaning of the sentence makes sense, we are not to look for nor concoct other meanings.

- We are not to spiritualize or allegorize scripture by assigning meanings to certain words or phrases when it's clear that the author, writing under the inspiration of the Holy Spirit, meant it to be understood just as it is written.
- **A literal hermeneutic allows the text to be the true authority.** It puts no power into the imagination of the interpreter (as an **allegorical** hermeneutic does).
- Although Revelation contains more symbolism than any other book, we can understand almost all of it with great confidence. As mentioned previously, the book often self-interprets its own symbols. But even when it does not, a comparison with other parts of scripture often yields the answers.
- The study of Revelation is not always easy but is immensely rewarding to the diligent student!

How Should Revelation Be Interpreted?

There are a number of different views concerning how Revelation should be interpreted. As already mentioned, the approach advocated for in this study involves a literal, grammatical, historical, contextual, or plain hermeneutic. A consistent literal hermeneutic always results in a **futuristic** view of Revelation (Chapters 4-22).

- **Futurism** – The idea that most of Revelation (Chapters 4-22) concerns future, literal events. This view is the outworking of a consistent application of the literal interpretive method. It follows the threefold outline of "the things you have seen (past), things that are (present), and things that are to come (future)" mentioned in Revelation 1:19.
- **Allegorism** – The idea that applies an allegorical or a mystical interpretation to the content of Revelation. Instead of interpreting the book to describe literal, future events, the allegorist understands it to depict the general spiritual struggle between the Church and evil. As a result, much of Revelation is interpreted subjectively according to the imagination of each interpreter.
- **Preterism** – The idea that the events presented in Revelation deal only with already fulfilled history (usually thought to be events in the first century AD, such as those involving the fall of Jerusalem and the Temple around 70 AD).
- **Partial Preterism** – The idea that the events presented in Revelation deal only with already fulfilled history, with the single exception being the Second Coming of Christ, which is viewed as a future event.
- **Historicism** – The idea that sees the events of Revelation as referring to church history, spanning from the apostles to the present. Historicists seek to identify events in church history and apply them to events described in Revelation.

Revelation's Authorship and Date of Composition

The writer of Revelation calls himself John (Revelation 1:1, 4, 9; 22:8). Since the time of the early Church, authorship of

Revelation has been overwhelmingly attributed to **John, the apostle and disciple of the Lord**. Internal and external evidence points strongly to the conclusion that Revelation was written around **95 AD** during the reign of the Roman emperor Domitian.

Revelation's Position in the Bible

In Genesis, we discover the beginning of all things. Meanwhile, Revelation presents the conclusion of all that began in Genesis. All prophetic themes of the Bible that are introduced in Genesis are brought to final consummation in Revelation. Several examples are:

- The creation of heaven and earth versus the creation of the new heaven and new earth.
- Satan's appearance as the ultimate villain versus Satan's final defeat.
- The rise of sin and death versus the ultimate defeat of sin and death.
- The way to the Tree of Life closed versus the way to the Tree of Life opened.
- The rise of Babylon versus the fall of Babylon.
- Man estranged from God versus man reconciled to God.
- The marriage of the first Adam versus the marriage of the Last Adam (Christ).
- Paradise lost versus paradise regained.

Revelation Is Meant to be Understood

Much of what is revealed to the Old Testament prophet Daniel is also disclosed in Revelation. But while Daniel was told that the words of the prophecy given to him were **sealed up** until the time of the end, John was told that Revelation was to remain **unsealed**, as the time of its fulfillment is imminent!

*"He said, 'Go your way, Daniel, **for the words are shut up and sealed until the time of the end.** Many shall purify themselves and make themselves white and be refined, but the wicked shall act wickedly. And none of the wicked shall understand, but those who are wise shall understand.'"*
-Daniel 12:9-10 (ESV)

*"And he said to me, '**Do not seal up the words of the prophecy of this book, for the time is near.** Let the evildoer still do evil, and the filthy still be filthy, and the righteous still do right, and the holy still be holy.'"*
-Revelation 22:10-11 (ESV)

The Purpose of Revelation

- To reveal Jesus, His deity, His power, and His glory.
- To reveal God's plan and action in the last days.
- To reveal that Jesus Christ wins the victory and that the Church will enjoy the paradise of heaven for eternity.
- To exhort us toward spiritual readiness for Christ's return!

The Major Divisions of Revelation

- Chapter 1 – The Revelation of Jesus Christ.
- Chapters 2-3 – The Church Age (unknown duration).
- Chapters 4-19 – The Judgment Phase of the Day of the Lord (culminates in a final seven-year period often called the Tribulation).

6

- Chapter 20 – The Kingdom Age/Millennial Kingdom (one thousand years).
- Chapters 21-22 – The Eternal State (time as we know it is no more).

Is Revelation Chronological?

A number of reasons indicate that Revelation should be understood as chronological in terms of the flow of its narrative. The text is full of phrases such as "after these things" and "after this," which clearly denote sequential order. Further, the Seal, Trumpet, and Bowl Judgments are each denoted by "first, second, third, etc.," indicating a sequence.

However, there are at least five notable "parenthetical" sections that pause the chronology in order to provide deeper explanation of certain concepts and events. These parenthetical segments are often inserted between the sixth and seventh judgments of each type (Seals, Trumpets, Bowls).

- **Chapter 7**, which describes the sealing of 144,000 Jewish evangelists, is parenthetically inserted between the Sixth and Seventh Seals.
- **Chapters 10:1-11:13**, which describe the "small scroll" and the Two Witnesses, are parenthetically inserted between the Sixth and Seventh Trumpets.
- **Chapters 12-14**, which describe the Woman and the Dragon, Satan's eviction from heaven, Israel's flight to the wilderness, the two Beasts, the Lamb and the 144,000, the messages of the three angels, and the harvest of the earth, are parenthetically inserted between the Seventh Trumpet and the pouring of the Seven Bowls.
- **Chapter 16:13-16**, which describes three unclean spirits gathering the nations for war at Armageddon,

is parenthetically inserted between the Sixth and
Seventh Bowls.

- **Chapters 17:1-19:10**, which describe the fall of
  Babylon and the subsequent rejoicing in heaven, are
  parenthetically inserted between the Seventh Bowl
  and the Second Coming of Christ to the earth.

Notes

2

THE REVELATION OF JESUS CHRIST
REVELATION CHAPTER 1

The Prologue – Chapter 1:1-3

> *"The revelation of Jesus Christ, which God gave him to show to his servants the things that must soon take place. He made it known by sending his angel to his servant John, who bore witness to the word of God and to the testimony of Jesus Christ, even to all that he saw. Blessed is the one who reads aloud the words of this prophecy, and blessed are those who hear, and who keep what is written in it, for the time is near."*
> -Revelation 1:1-3 (ESV)

- Two interpretations of the opening phrase "the revelation of Jesus Christ" have been suggested based on the question "Who or what is getting revealed?" Is it saying that Jesus is the One being revealed, or is it saying that He is the One doing the revealing? The authors of this study believe both are true. Revelation of course provides a detailed disclosure of the futuristic happenings that will climax in Jesus's physical coming in the clouds (His revealing or revelation). But we must not overlook the prominence the book places on the revelation or unveiling of the true identity of Jesus.

- Revelation is transmitted from God to Jesus Christ, to His angel, and then to John – to then be conveyed to "His servants," or the Church.
- Revelation reveals what will come to pass in the last days. It is that which must soon (meaning imminently) come to pass. That which the prophet Daniel said would occur "in the latter days" (Daniel 2:28) is here described as that which "must soon take place."
- A blessing is pronounced upon those who read, hear, and keep the words written in the book. The book of Revelation both begins and ends with a promise of blessing.

*"And behold, I am coming soon. **Blessed** is the one who keeps the words of the prophecy of this book."*
-Revelation 22:7 (ESV)

The Salutation – Chapter 1:4-8

The Book Was Written to the Church
(Verses 4-6)

"John to the seven churches that are in Asia: Grace to you and peace from him who is and who was and who is to come, and from the seven spirits who are before his throne, and from Jesus Christ the faithful witness, the firstborn of the dead, and the ruler of kings on earth. To him who loves us and has freed us from our sins by his blood and made us a kingdom, priests to his God and Father, to him be glory and dominion forever and ever. Amen."

-Revelation 1:4-6 (ESV)

- The immediate recipients of Revelation were seven churches located in Asia Minor, but the book contains information relevant to all churches throughout the present Church Age. The same issues that affected these seven churches are the same issues that affect churches today.
- Chapters 2 and 3 deal with issues related to the Church and are just as critical to our understanding as the subsequent futuristic chapters of Revelation (maybe even more so, since they are directly applicable to us today). They warn the Church of sins and sinful conditions that negatively affect our relationship with Jesus Christ and threaten our readiness for His imminent coming.
- The "seven spirits who are before His throne" may be a reference to the seven-fold Spirit of God described in Isaiah 11:2 (discussed later).

The Glorious Announcement
(Verse 7)

*"Behold, **he is coming with the clouds**, and every eye will see him, even those who **pierced him**, and all tribes of the earth will wail on account of him. Even so. Amen."*
-Revelation 1:7 (ESV)

- Verse 7 describes the topic of the entire book: the Second Coming of Jesus Christ, which culminates with His return to the earth at the end of the Tribulation to establish His Millennial Kingdom!
- This idea of "coming with the clouds" is foretold much earlier in Daniel 7:13-14, where Daniel is

shown the Son of Man's future coming to conquer the wicked and receive an everlasting Kingdom.

*"I saw in the night visions, and behold, **with the clouds of heaven there came one like a son of man**, and he came to the Ancient of Days and was presented before him. **And to him was given dominion and glory and a kingdom**, that all peoples, nations, and languages should serve him; his dominion is an **everlasting dominion, which shall not pass away, and his kingdom one that shall not be destroyed."***
  -Daniel 7:13-14 (ESV)

- The second part of Revelation 1:7 describes His coming as being witnessed by all, including "those who pierced him" (the nation of Israel) and mentions them wailing and mourning on account of Him. This was foretold much earlier in Zechariah 12:10.

*"And I will pour out on the house of David and the inhabitants of Jerusalem a spirit of grace and pleas for mercy, so that, **when they look on me, on him whom they have pierced, they shall mourn for him**, as one mourns for an only child, and weep bitterly over him, as one weeps over a firstborn."*
  -Zechariah 12:10 (ESV)

Jesus Christ – The Almighty God of Past, Present, and Future
(Verse 8)

"'I am the Alpha and the Omega,' says the Lord God, 'who is and who was and who is to come, the Almighty.'"
  -Revelation 1:8 (ESV)

- Here, we find a powerful declaration revealing the true identity of Jesus Christ as the one God of eternity. He is called the "Alpha and the Omega" (the first and last letters of the Greek alphabet), referring to His eternal existence as God.

- The subject of Verse 8 is certainly Jesus, as we find this statement repeated in Verse 11. Verse 13 then identifies the speaker in Verse 11 as the Son of Man.
- The same language is also used later on in Revelation 22:13 when also speaking of Jesus.

"Behold, I am coming soon, bringing my recompense with me, to repay each one for what he has done. I am the Alpha and the Omega, the first and the last, the beginning and the end."
-Revelation 22:13 (ESV)

- Furthermore, this is also the same description given concerning the "One who sat on the throne" seen by John when he gets called up to heaven in Chapter 4.

"At once I was in the Spirit, and behold, a throne stood in heaven, with one seated on the throne. ... And the four living creatures, each of them with six wings, are full of eyes all around and within, and day and night they never cease to say, 'Holy, holy, holy, is the Lord God Almighty, who was and is and is to come!'"
-Revelation 4:2 and 8 (ESV)

The Vision of the Glorified Christ – Chapter 1:9-20

The Backdrop of the Vision
(Verses 9-11)

- The apostle John had been banished to the isle of Patmos, an island in the Aegean Sea off the coast of Asia Minor (modern-day Turkey). John was exiled there by the Roman emperor Domitian around 95 AD. Patmos was a rocky, barren island that Rome used as a sort of "prison island."

- The Revelation begins with John being "in the Spirit on the Lord's day." Some believe "the Lord's day" refers to Sunday, the day on which the early Christians would gather to worship in memorial of Christ's resurrection on this day. In other words, John was in the Spirit on a Sunday when he received this vision. Others believe it to be a reference to the Biblical "Day of the Lord," which was the setting of John's vision (Chapters 4-22). In other words, John was in the Spirit and was given a vision of the Day of the Lord.

Jesus Is in the Midst of His Churches
(Verses 12-16)

- After hearing the voice like a trumpet, John turned and was given a glimpse of Jesus Christ in His full deity.
- John also sees seven golden lamp stands. This symbolism is explained in Verse 20. They represent the seven churches, which makes sense since churches are intended to be a light in the world.
- The Son of Man (Jesus Christ) is pictured as standing in the midst of the seven golden lamp stands. Jesus is in the midst of His churches!
- In His right hand, Jesus held seven stars. This symbolism is also explained in Verse 20. The stars represent the angels of the seven churches. Most believe that in this particular context, these seven angels are the seven human leaders of the seven churches. The

word angel in Greek means "a messenger, one who is sent." In several other instances in the New Testament, this term is also used to refer to human messengers (Matthew 11:10; Mark 1:2; Luke 7:24, 27; 9:52). True leaders of the Church are held in Jesus's hand!

- Each of the letters to the seven churches in Chapters 2-3 begin with Jesus telling John: "To the angel of the church in ..., write ... " This further indicates that the seven messengers being spoken of are likely the human pastors or leaders, who would then convey the message to their congregations.

John Was Commissioned to Write
(Verses 17-20)

*"When I saw him, I fell at his feet as though dead. But he laid his right hand on me, saying, 'Fear not, I am the first and the last, and the living one. I died, and behold I am alive forevermore, and I have the keys of Death and Hades. **Write therefore the things that you have seen, those that are and those that are to take place after this.**'"*
-Revelation 1:17-19 (ESV)

- After seeing this powerful sight, John collapsed in fear. Jesus then told John not to fear and identified Himself yet again as the first and the last who died but is alive forevermore (a description given repeatedly throughout the book).
- Jesus then gave John the following commission: to write "the things that you **have seen,** those that **are** and those that **are to take place after this.**" This statement contains the key to understanding Revelation. It acts as a threefold outline of the book as a whole, separating the content into "things seen"

(past), "things that are" (present), and "things that are to take place after this" (future).

By recognizing this outline, our understanding of Revelation is made clear:

- The "things seen" are those that we've just studied in Chapter 1.
- The "things that are" refer to Chapters 2-3, which contain the seven messages of Christ written to the seven churches that were in existence during John's lifetime and still bear relevance to churches today. In other words, this refers to the Church Age that was in existence at the time the vision was given and is still active today.
- The "things that are to take place after this" include the future, prophetic events described in Chapters 4-22 after the conclusion of the Church Age. The Greek phrase is *meta tauta*, which literally means "after these things." This is important, as Chapter 4 begins with this exact phrase *meta tauta*, clueing us into the fact that John was beginning the prophetic, futuristic portion of the book.
- This threefold outline allows Revelation to speak for itself and neatly organize its own content without the readers imposing their own views from the outside.
- This recognition establishes a futurist interpretation of the bulk of the book.

Notes

3

THE LETTERS TO THE SEVEN CHURCHES

REVELATION CHAPTERS 2 TO 3

Overview

Chapters 2 and 3 include seven epistles (or letters) written to seven real first century churches located in Asia Minor (modern-day Turkey). These churches were based in Ephesus, Smyrna, Pergamum, Thyatira, Sardis, Philadelphia, and Laodicea. All of these cities were situated relatively close to the island of Patmos, where John wrote Revelation. Each church's message, though specific to its own circumstances, also offers applications for our lives and our churches today.

The Purpose of Writing to the Churches

- These letters to the churches seem to have a threefold application.
- Naturally, they apply to the actual first century churches to which they were addressed.
- They also apply to the conditions present within all churches throughout the Church Age.

- Additionally, some also speculate that they may prophetically represent historical time periods of the Church Age. For example, the church of Ephesus (the first letter) would resemble the early Church, while Laodicea (the seventh letter) represents today's lukewarm churches.

Why These Seven Churches?

- The number seven is God's number for completion (e.g., seven days of creation, seven days in a week). The number seven is prominently used throughout Revelation.
- Writing to the seven churches neatly represents the complete Church Age and the issues that face the Church to this day.

The Structure of the Letters

- John was told to write what Jesus declared to each of the churches.
- While each letter concerns distinctive aspects of the individual church to which it was written, there are similarities among all seven.
- Each letter begins with the words "I know your works."
- Each letter ends with a promise to those who overcome.
- Each letter has the same concluding sentence: "He who has an ear, let him hear what the Spirit says to the churches."
- The letters each contain a commendation (with the exception of Sardis and Laodicea). It pointed out what each church was doing well.

- The letters each contain a reprimand (with the exception of Smyrna and Philadelphia). It pointed out what each church was doing poorly and included a warning and a call to repentance. Each was given a challenge to make the necessary corrective action.
- In each letter, the urgency to take repentant action is based upon the imminent (any moment) return of the Lord.

The Church in Ephesus – Chapter 2:1-7

"The Loveless Church"

The church in Ephesus was commended for their good works, their patient endurance, their intolerance of evil, and the way they hated the deeds of the Nicolaitans and rejected their teachings.

Note: The Nicolaitans appear to be a group who claimed to be Christian but advocated participation in pagan worship and immoral activities.

The complaint against this church was that they had left their first love (their love for God and for each other). They were warned to repent and turn back to their initial heartfelt affection for the Lord; otherwise, He would "remove their lamp-stand from its place." Some believe this just meant the removal of their testimony, while others believe it represented a much more dire consequence (losing their status as a church).

The promise to the overcomer was access to the Tree of Life!

The Church in Smyrna – Chapter 2:8-11

"The Persecuted Church"

The church in Smyrna had endured much persecution and was one of only two churches to which Jesus offered no rebuke. He instead declared that He knew their works of service and their sufferings. He also said that He knew their poverty, but that they actually were rich spiritually.

This church had faith even in the midst of their tribulations. They were encouraged not to be fearful regarding the things they were yet to suffer, and that their suffering would be short.

Note: The "tribulation" being experienced by this church refers to the general troubles that have been experienced throughout the Church Age and throughout time. It does not refer to the Tribulation spoken of in the later futuristic part of Revelation. This seven-year Tribulation is the time of the wrath of God that the Church will not experience.

The double promise was a crown of life and the assurance that the victorious would not be harmed by the Second Death (the Lake of Fire).

The Church in Pergamos – Chapter 2:12-17

"The Worldly Church"

This church was located in a city that was home to much idolatry and pagan religion (Jesus refers to it here as "where Satan has his throne" and "where Satan lives"). Although the church in Pergamos had remained faithful to Jesus, they had also allowed in many false doctrines and tolerated those who engaged in such teaching. They had begun to lose their separation from the world. The warning to this church was to repent; otherwise, the Lord would fight against them with the sword of His mouth.

The promise to the overcomer was the promise of hidden manna – heavenly nourishment that the world knows nothing about – and a white stone, symbolizing the acquittal of the accused.

The Church in Thyatira – Chapter 2:18-29

"The Paganized Church"

Thyatira was a city full of pagan worship. The church in Thyatira was commended for being a church of good works. Jesus recognized their growth in love, service, and patience. But the rebuke against this church was that they tolerated the false prophetess Jezebel (a reference to the Old Testament story of King Ahab's wife, who took Israel to a deeper level of idolatry and immorality). Apparently, in this same way, the Thyatiran church had allowed an individual who was teaching things contrary to true doctrine into a place of leadership and prominence. Jesus warned of severe punishment to those who would not repent.

The promise to the overcomer was that they would share in the true authority of Christ in the coming Kingdom.

The Church in Sardis – Chapter 3:1-6

"The Lifeless Church"

Sardis was a city noted for its wealth from its prosperous textile and jewelry industries. The rebuke against this church was that, while they had a reputation for spirituality, they had actually become spiritually deadened. However, even in this environment there were those who had a genuine relationship with Jesus Christ.

The exhortation to this church was to wake up, to strengthen what remained, and to recover and keep the Word of God. They were warned to repent; otherwise, they would experience judgment instead of blessing when the Lord comes.

The promise to those who repent was both a reward of eternal life and an escape from judgment ("I will not blot your name from the Book of Life").

The Church in Philadelphia – Chapter 3:7-13

"The Faithful Church"

Along with the church in Smyrna, the church in Philadelphia was the other of only two churches to receive no rebuke from the Lord. The church in this city was noted for its missionary efforts and faithful witness to God's Word, while not denying His name. The promise and blessing they were given are based on two conditions: obedience to the Word and devotion to the name of Jesus.

A key promise given to this church was "I will keep you from the hour of testing that is going to come on the whole world ..." This clearly denotes a pretribulational timing to Jesus's promise of the Rapture of the Church. They were promised to not experience any part of the coming judgments of the Day of the Lord. Notice that it doesn't say they would be preserved through it, but rather, that they would be kept from that time altogether.

The Church in Laodicea – Chapter 3:14-22

"The Lukewarm Church"

Jesus gave no commendation at all to this church, which was located in the proud and wealthy city of Laodicea. He calls them a "lukewarm" church, illustrating their dangerous spiritual condition of being neither hot nor cold. Christ warned them that He would vomit them out of His mouth due to this lukewarm state.

The Laodicean church had mistaken their wealth and physical comforts for God's blessing. They had actually regressed to the point where Jesus was pictured as standing at the door desiring to come in (meaning He was outside of the church looking in, instead of being inside in their midst).

The promise of eternal relationship was given to those who repent and overcome. The overcomers were promised the right to sit with Christ on His throne.

Notes

4

THE THRONE ROOM IN HEAVEN
REVELATION CHAPTERS 4 TO 5

The Scene in Heaven – Chapter 4

The Present Shifts to the Future
(Verse 1)

"After this [meta tauta] *I looked, and behold, a door standing open in heaven! And the first voice, which I had heard speaking to me like a trumpet, said, 'Come up here, and* **I will show you what must take place** *after this* [meta tauta].'"
-Revelation 4:1 (ESV)

As Chapter 3 ends and Chapter 4 begins, the setting shifts from the second division of Revelation ("the things that **are**" – the letters to the seven churches that were on the earth during John's day) to the third ("things that are **yet to come**" – the futuristic part of the book).

As mentioned, we note this in Greek through the phrase *meta tauta*, which always indicates a new part of the vision. In this case, it further indicates a new section of the book, marking the transition from the Church Age context to the futuristic context. John is now brought into heaven, where he sees a vision of God's eschatological program called the Day of the Lord, followed by the Eternal State.

Note: Eschatology is the study of the "last things" (Greek: *eschatos*), or the end-times.

The Rapture of the Church

- John's summons to heaven has been seen by many as a type of the **Rapture** (or supernatural "catching away") of the Church since that event will happen just prior to the events about to be shown to him. In other words, "after this" (after the Church Age, or the present-tense division of Revelation in Chapters 2-3), John was "raptured" from Earth to heaven to witness what would take place after the actual Rapture of the Church occurs.

- A door was opened in heaven (Rapture imagery) and a voice like a trumpet was heard (Cross-reference with 1 Thessalonians 4:16, part of the most well-known Rapture passage in the Bible, which speaks of a shout, the voice of the archangel, and the sound of a trumpet).

- Notice also that throughout Chapters 4 to 19, the Church is never again mentioned. Contrast that with the fact that the Church is mentioned nineteen times prior to Chapter 4. It would seem that this conspicuous absence is due to the fact that the Rapture chronologically takes place here, as represented by John being caught up to heaven to witness the events that follow. After the Rapture, the

Church is no longer on earth and the Church Age is over.

- The Rapture is the forceful "catching away" promised to the Church (1 Thessalonians 4:13-18). It is an imminent rescue from imminent judgment (1 Thessalonians 1:9-10), it is our comforting promise (1 Thessalonians 4:18), and it is our blessed hope (Titus 2:13).

Rapture Timing Views

- **Posttribulationalism** – The idea that the Church will go through the entire Tribulation and be raptured at the end.
- **Midtribulationalism** – The idea that the Church will go through the first half of the Tribulation and then be raptured at the midpoint.
- **Prewrath Rapturism** – The idea that the entire Tribulation is not part of God's wrath. The Church will be raptured during the Tribulation, but prior to the segment that begins God's wrath. Typical prewrath schemes place this about three-quarters of the way through the Tribulation.
- **Pretribulationalism** – The idea that the Church will be raptured prior to the Tribulation and therefore will not be on Earth to experience any of its judgments.

The Rapture Versus The Second Coming

It is critical to distinguish the Rapture from the Second Coming of Christ. As mentioned, the Rapture is the supernatural catching away of the Church to meet Jesus Christ in the air. At this time, we will be given glorified bodies and will be brought to His Father's house in heaven. The central passages dealing with the Rapture are John 14:1-3, 1 Thessalonians 4:13-18, and 1 Corinthians 15:51-58.

The Second Coming is when Jesus Christ physically returns to the earth at the end of the Tribulation. Every eye sees Him, and He sets foot on the Mount of Olives in Jerusalem. It is primarily associated with Christ's judgment of the wicked. The central passages dealing with Christ's Second Coming to the earth are Isaiah 63:1-6, Zechariah 14:1-21, Matthew 24:29-31, Mark 13:24-27, Luke 21:25-27, Jude 1:14-15, and Revelation 19.

Note: In the Bible, it is important to recognize that both the Rapture and the Second Coming are events that are included within Christ's broader *Parousia*. This Greek word means "coming or presence" and is the word the New Testament uses to variously refer to the Rapture and the Second Coming, and encompasses all of the events that take place in between (Matthew 24:3, 27, 37; 1 Corinthians 15:23; 1 Thessalonians 2:19; 3:13; 4:15; 5:23; 2 Thessalonians 2:1, 8; James 5:7-8; 2 Peter 1:16; 3:4; 1 John 2:28). This entire period makes up Christ's future Parousia (or Second Advent), though the events related to it occur within a certain sequence. To avoid confusion, we will hereafter refer to Christ's Second Coming to the earth at the end of the Tribulation specifically as the "Second Coming proper." More will be said of this as we continue.

While the Rapture and the Second Coming proper may bear some similarities, it is their notable differences that help us recognize them as distinct events within Christ's broader Parousia. The following are just several of the differences:

- The Rapture may occur at any moment without preconditions. There are no signs preceding it. The Second Coming proper takes place at the end of a sequence of specific events. It is preceded by numerous signs.

- At the Rapture, the Church is rescued from the imminent period of judgment that Christ will bring upon the wicked world (the broad Day of the Lord). At the Second Coming proper, Jesus returns at the end of this period to execute the climax of this judgment.
- At the Rapture, Jesus comes to catch away His Church and bring them to His Father's house in heaven. At the Second Coming proper, Jesus comes to the earth bringing His Church with Him.
- The Rapture (and the Church as a whole) are mystery New Testament revelations. The Second Coming proper was known of and expected throughout the Old Testament prophets.

The Heavenly Throne Room
(Verses 2-3)

After a door is opened in heaven and John hears a voice as a trumpet saying, "Come up here," he is immediately transported into the throne room of God in heaven.

- John sees **One** sitting on the throne, full of glory.
- Something like a sea of glass lay before the throne, and a rainbow surrounded it.

Twenty-Four Elders Sitting on Twenty-Four Thrones
(Verse 4)

Around the throne of God, John saw twenty-four "elders" who sat on twenty-four thrones. These beings wore white garments and had on golden crowns.

- The Twenty-Four Elders seem to represent the Church. Alternatively, some have speculated that they represent the saints of all ages (twelve sons of Jacob plus twelve apostles). Another view is that they comprise a special class of angelic beings.

- The Twenty-Four Elders have on white robes, wear golden crowns, and sit on thrones. In the letters to the seven churches, the overcomers of the Church Age were promised white garments (Revelation 3:5), crowns (Revelation 3:11), and thrones (Revelation 3:21).

- The Twenty-Four Elders worship and sing the song of the redeemed. The KJV has them singing in the first person, while other translations have them singing in the third person. If the KJV is correct, then they definitely cannot be angels or heavenly beings.

- In Revelation 5:9-10, they cry: "Thou art worthy to take the book, and to open the seals thereof: for thou wast slain, and hast redeemed **us** to God by thy blood **out of every kindred, and tongue, and people, and nation;** and hast made **us** unto our God **kings and priests:** and **we shall reign on the earth**" (KJV). Revelation 1:5-6 and 1 Peter 2:9 describe the Church as being kings and priests unto God. The Church is the only group that is purchased by the blood of the Lamb and is taken from every nation and people group to become kings and priests who will reign on the earth.

- Notice that if the Twenty-Four Elders do represent the raptured Church in heaven, it means they are there with Christ in heaven prior to any of the wrathful judgments being poured out upon the earth (necessitating a pretribulation Rapture view).

The Seven Spirits of God
(Verse 5)

From the throne came flashes of lightning, rumblings and thundering. In front of the throne were seven burning candlesticks, which are the seven spirits of God. Before the throne there was a sea of glass, like crystal.

The seven spirits of God are symbolized here as seven burning lamps that are before God's throne. This picture agrees with the Old Testament prophet Zechariah's vision, in which he sees the Holy Spirit symbolized as a golden lampstand with a bowl at the top and seven lamps on it (Zechariah 4:2).

Isaiah 11:2 also references the Holy Spirit using a seven-fold description (the Spirit of the Lord, the Spirit of wisdom, the Spirit of understanding, the Spirit of counsel, the Spirit of might, the Spirit of knowledge, and the Spirit of the fear of the Lord).

The Four Beasts
(Verses 6-11)

Also around the throne are four beasts (or "living creatures"), full of eyes in the front and in the back.

- Each has a different appearance: lion, calf, man, and eagle (Cross-reference with the four living creatures of Ezekiel 1, and possibly the seraphim in Isaiah 6).
- They worship the One on the throne continually, saying "Holy, holy, holy, Lord God Almighty, who was and is and is to come!"

The Seven-Sealed Scroll and the Lamb – Chapter 5

The Seven-Sealed Scroll
(Verses 1-5)

The One John saw sitting on the throne held a scroll with writing on the inside and the outside, and was sealed with seven seals. An angel proclaimed, "Who is worthy to open the scroll and loose the seals?" John wept because no one was found worthy.

- Based on the description given, this scroll was typical of an ancient title deed. It would appear that this scroll was a title deed to all of the earth. It revealed the sordid story of loss, bondage, and the enslavement of humanity due to sin.
- The scroll was not just sealed, as was the custom, but was sealed with a total of seven seals. Only a qualified redeemer was able to break the seals, open the scroll, and redeem those who were enslaved.

The Lamb Takes the Scroll
(Verses 6-14)

When John began to weep, one of the elders said, "Do not weep. Behold, the Lion of the tribe of Judah, the Root of David, has prevailed to open the scroll and to loose the seven seals." John turned to look at the Lion of the tribe of Judah but saw a Lamb appearing as though it had been slain.

- The Lamb had seven horns and seven eyes, which are the seven Spirits of God. The Lamb took the scroll and the heavens were filled with worship.

- As a "kinsman of Adam" and a true sinless man, the Lamb alone (picturing Jesus Christ in His redemptive role) was found worthy to open the seals and redeem mankind and the earth! We have redemption through His blood and new life by His Spirit. John the Baptist's declaration rings down through the ages, "Behold the Lamb of God, which taketh away the sin of the world" (John 1:29, KJV).
- Then all of heaven rejoices and worships the Lamb, who is Jesus Christ!

The Wrath of the Lamb

As Jesus begins to open the seven seals on the scroll, His wrathful judgments begin to be poured out upon the wicked inhabitants left on the earth. **This occurs at the beginning of the broad period of the Day of the Lord.**

Note: The Day of the Lord is a frequently used Biblical term that, in its eschatological sense, refers to the future time when God will intervene in human history in order to judge sin, judge His enemies, accomplish His purposes for mankind, and display His sovereignty. Biblically, this future Day of the Lord has a **double sense** in terms of duration. In its **broad** sense, it refers to a prolonged period that begins with the Rapture and concludes with the end of the Millennial Kingdom. But in its **narrow** sense, it refers to a specific day of culmination in which Christ returns in glory to judge His enemies. This narrow period is sometimes called "the great and terrible Day of the Lord," referring to the time immediately surrounding the Second Coming proper (when Christ physically returns to the earth at the end of the Tribulation). So, the Day of the Lord is a broad period but yet it also has a culminating day (similar to the Christmas season versus Christmas Day).

The outpouring of divine wrath begins as Jesus opens the Seal Judgments. All those who were unraptured were left behind to experience this wrath. Remember, the Church is in heaven with Christ (likely represented by John and/or the Twenty-Four Elders) while Jesus begins to pour out the first judgments. The Church is not on earth to experience any of it! Paul refers to this in 1 Thessalonians 1:10, as he speaks of the Church presently awaiting the return of Jesus Christ from heaven – the event that would feature their rescue (the Rapture) from the oncoming wrath of the broad Day of the Lord.

"And to wait for his Son from heaven, whom he raised from the dead, even Jesus, which delivered us from the wrath to come."
-1 Thessalonians 1:10 (KJV)

This wrath that is unleashed as Jesus opens the seals initiates the broad period of the Day of the Lord. Paul comments further in 1 Thessalonians 5.

"But of the times and the seasons, brethren, ye have no need that I write unto you. For yourselves know perfectly that the day of the Lord so cometh as a thief in the night. For when they shall say, Peace and safety; then sudden destruction cometh upon them, as travail upon a woman with child; and they shall not escape. But ye, brethren, are not in darkness, that that day should overtake you as a thief. Ye are all the children of light, and the children of the day: we are not of the night, nor of darkness. Therefore let us not sleep, as do others; but let us watch and be sober. For they that sleep sleep in the night; and they that be drunken are drunken in the night. But let us, who are of the day, be sober, putting on the breastplate of faith and love; and for an helmet, the hope of salvation. For God hath not appointed us to wrath, but to obtain salvation by our Lord Jesus Christ, ... Wherefore comfort yourselves together..."
-1 Thessalonians 5:1-9, 11a (KJV)

The judgment phase of the broad Day of the Lord (in which the subsequent judgments of Revelation take place) **culminates in a final period of seven years**, often called the **Tribulation** or **Daniel's seventieth week**. The Old Testament also calls this period "the time of Jacob's trouble" (Jeremiah 30:7).

Many believe that scripture implies a gap of time in between the Rapture and the Tribulation, though its potential duration is unknown. It may be a short period or one that lasts for a number of years. The only clue we have is from Jesus's statement in Matthew 24:34, in which He declares that a single generation would witness this entire broad period of judgment (the potential gap plus the seven-year Tribulation).

The Tribulation (or final "week of years") is the final seven-year segment that remains on Israel's prophetic calendar. This prophetic outline is given in Daniel 9:24-27, and is often called Daniel's "seventy weeks prophecy" (the chronological backbone of Bible prophecy).

"**Seventy weeks** are determined upon thy people and upon thy holy city, to finish the transgression, and to make an end of sins, and to make reconciliation for iniquity, and to bring in everlasting righteousness, and to seal up the vision and prophecy, and to anoint the most Holy. Know therefore and understand, that from the going forth of the commandment to restore and to build Jerusalem unto the Messiah the Prince shall be **seven weeks, and threescore and two weeks**: the street shall be built again, and the wall, even in troublous times. And after threescore and two weeks shall Messiah be cut off, but not for himself: and the people of the prince that shall come shall destroy the city and the sanctuary; and the end thereof shall be with a flood, and unto the end of the war desolations are determined. And he shall confirm the covenant with many for **one week**: and in the midst of the week he shall cause the sacrifice and the oblation to cease, and for the overspreading of abomina-

tions he shall make it desolate, even until the consummation, and that determined shall be poured upon the desolate."
  -Daniel 9:24-27 (KJV)

- The prophecy specifically concerns the Jews and Jerusalem (Verse 1, "thy people and ... thy holy city").
- It mentions a period of **seven** weeks (or heptads) of years, plus a consecutive period of **sixty-two** weeks of years (which equals **sixty-nine** weeks of years, or four hundred ninety years) that would run until the Messiah's coming. In Verse 25, this period was given a specific beginning point ("from the going forth of the commandment to restore and to build Jerusalem") and a specific ending point ("unto the Messiah the Prince"). In other words, from the decree to rebuild Jerusalem until the Messiah's coming will be four hundred ninety years.
- After the **sixty-nine** weeks but before the **seventieth** week, the Messiah would be cut off (killed), which took place at the crucifixion of Christ in 33 AD.
- The fact that the Messiah's death was said to follow the **sixty-ninth** week but precede the **seventieth** week necessitates the existence of a gap in between the two. This gap of time primarily involves the present Church Age.
- One final week (a **seventieth** week, the Tribulation) still remains (Verse 27, "And he shall confirm the covenant with many for one week ..."). The Antichrist's confirmation of a covenant acts as the beginning point of this final week.
- At the midpoint of this week, he causes the "sacrifice and the oblation to cease" (the Jewish Temple rituals).
- At the end point, the Second Coming proper occurs.

Notes

5

THE OPENING OF THE SEVEN SEALS
REVELATION CHAPTERS 6 TO 8:5

The Lamb Opens the Seals – Chapter 6

"Now I watched when the Lamb opened one of the seven seals, and I heard one of the four living creatures say with a voice like thunder, 'Come!'"

-Revelation 6:1 (ESV)

Chapter 6 begins with Jesus Christ, the Lamb of God, beginning to open the Seven Seals. Each releases a judgment of wrath upon the wicked world as the broad Day of the Lord begins.

The Opening of the First Seal
(Verses 1-2)

The First Seal is opened, and a white horse with a rider having a crown and a bow but no arrows goes out conquering and to conquer.

- This seems to picture the Antichrist's initial rise to power. He is the counterfeit rider on a white horse, as contrasted with the coming of Christ in Chapter 19, where Christ is also pictured as coming on a white horse.
- Having a bow but no arrows may indicate that the Antichrist initially arrives onto the scene without war and violence but under the false banner of peace.
- Could the Rapture of the Church and the ensuing chaos open the door for the rise of the Antichrist? What societal effects will occur when millions of people suddenly vanish?
- Cross-reference this First Seal with Jesus's "birth pangs" description of the emergence of false messiahs that would deceive many (Matthew 24:5). The Antichrist (which in Greek means "pseudo-Christ") is the ultimate false messiah figure.

The Opening of the Second Seal
(Verses 3-4)

The Second Seal is opened, and a rider on a red horse comes forth. He is given a sword and power to conquer by war and take peace from the earth.

- Red is also the color of the Dragon in Revelation 12, which is Satan.
- This rider takes peace from the earth as terrible wars break out.
- Cross-reference this Second Seal with Jesus's "birth pangs" description of wars, rumors of wars, and nation rising against nation (Matthew 24:6-7).

The Opening of the Third Seal

46

(Verses 5-6)

The Third Seal is opened, and a rider on a black horse comes forth, carrying a scale for measuring the limited food supply.

- The balances held by the rider portray famine and scarcity. This is also represented by the black color of the horse, which symbolizes suffering. Famine is a typical result of the great wars that were described under the previous judgment.
- Wheat and barley were food staples in the ancient world, although wheat was a better grain than barley, and therefore costlier. A denarius was the standard silver coin in the Roman empire. One denarius was the average daily wage for a common worker. When this judgment occurs, the bare necessities for survival will cost a whole day's wages.
- The scarcity will apparently not be universal, as oil and wine will not be affected. Oil and wine were more luxurious items than wheat and barley in the ancient world. This may imply that while the common man is hurt by this famine, the rich (or world elite) are unhurt.
- Cross-reference this Third Seal with Jesus's "birth pangs" description of famine (Matthew 24:7).

The Opening of the Fourth Seal
(Verses 7-8)

The Fourth Seal is opened, and a rider on a pale horse (the Greek word is *chloros*, meaning pale green) comes forth, bringing death to a fourth part of the earth through violence, pestilence, famine, and wild beasts.

- The rider is pictured as Death, with Hades (the abode of the dead) following it.
- The current estimated population of the world is around eight billion. If using today's population, around two billion people would die.
- Cross-reference this Fourth Seal with Jesus's "birth pangs" description of death through famine, pestilence, and earthquakes (Matthew 24:7).

The Opening of the Fifth Seal
(Verses 9-11)

The Fifth Seal is opened, revealing those who have been martyred for the Lord. The viewpoint shifts from earth to heaven, as John sees those who have been killed for their faith in Christ.

- The martyrs cry for vengeance, but the Lord tells them to wait, for there will be others that will join their number. White robes are given to them, and they are told to rest a while.
- The judgment of this seal is the promise that the Lord will avenge their blood.
- The introduction of these martyrs at this juncture would indicate that their martyrdoms would have taken place as a result of what was taking place on the earth at this time.
- Cross-reference this Fifth Seal with Jesus's description of the persecution of believers during this time (Matthew 24:9).

The Opening of the Sixth Seal
(Verses 12-17)

The Sixth Seal is opened, and a catastrophic earthquake brings massive destruction to the planet. This earthquake shakes the whole earth and affects life globally.

- People both great and small hide, seeking cover in the rocks and mountains. They correctly recognize that these judgments are a result of the wrath of the Lamb, saying to the rocks, "Fall on us and hide us from the face of him who is seated on the throne, and from the wrath of the Lamb, for the great day of their wrath **has come**, and who can stand?" (Revelation 6:16b-17, ESV). The wicked of the earth now recognize that what they've been experiencing all along have been the judgments of the broad Day of the Lord. We should note that the Greek verb translated "has come" is aorist indicative, denoting the **previous arrival** of this great period of wrath.
- Their reference to "the great day" relates to the frequent Old Testament mentions of the Day of the Lord (Joel 2:11, 31; Zephaniah 1:14; Malachi 4:5). This period is frequently mentioned in the New Testament as well (Matthew 7:22; 1 Thessalonians 5:2, 2; 2 Peter 3:10).

The Sealing of the 144,000 and the Tribulation Saints – Chapter 7

To understand the book of Revelation, the reader must be mindful of the **five parenthetical insertions** located throughout the book (as mentioned earlier). Chapter 7 is the first of these parenthetical insertions, pausing between the Sixth and Seventh Seals in order to provide explanatory information concerning other events happening at this time.

The 144,000 Jewish Evangelists
(Verses 1-8)

"And I heard the number of the sealed, 144,000, sealed from every tribe of the sons of Israel."
-Revelation 7:4 (ESV)

As Chapter 7 begins, there is a pause prior to the opening of the Seventh Seal Judgment in order for God to seal 144,000 Jewish evangelists for their unique ministry. Four angels hold back the activity on the earth until the 144,000 are sealed. There are 12,000 sealed from each tribe of Israel.

The Great Multitude of Martyred Tribulation Saints
(Verses 9-17)

After this, John witnesses a great multitude standing before the throne of God who were clothed in white robes and holding palm branches. One of the elders tells John that these are the martyred saints which have come out of great tribulation.

"Then one of the elders addressed me, saying, 'Who are these, clothed in white robes, and from where have they come?' I said to him, 'Sir, you know.' And he said to me, 'These are the ones coming out of the great tribulation. They have washed their robes and made them white in the blood of the Lamb.'"
-Revelation 7:13-14 (ESV)

This ends the first parenthetical segment of Revelation, as the narrative will now continue with the opening of the Seventh Seal.

The Seventh Seal Unleashes the Seven Trumpet Judgments – Chapter 8:1-5

The Opening of the Seventh Seal
(Verses 1-5)

"When the Lamb opened the seventh seal, there was silence in heaven for about half an hour. Then I saw the seven angels who stand before God, and seven trumpets were given to them."
-Revelation 8:1-2 (ESV)

The Seventh Seal is opened, which unlocks the Seven Trumpet Judgments that are to follow. All of the worship and celebration in heaven stops in apparent anticipation of the next set of events.

- Seven angels are given seven trumpets.
- Another angel that had a golden vessel filled with the prayers of the saints comes and stands by the altar in heaven. The angel then throws the vessel to the earth and the result is chaos. There is noise, thunders, lightings, and an earthquake.
- The seven angels with the seven trumpets prepare to sound their trumpets and release each of the coming judgments.

Notes

6

THE SOUNDING OF THE SEVEN TRUMPETS

REVELATION CHAPTERS 8:6 TO 11

The First Six Trumpets Are Sounded – Chapters 8:6 to 9

"Now the seven angels who had the seven trumpets prepared to blow them."
-Revelation 8:6 (ESV)

The Sounding of the First Trumpet
(Verse 7)

The First Trumpet is sounded, and hail and fire mingled with blood are cast to the earth. One-third of the trees and green grass are burned up.

The Sounding of the Second Trumpet
(Verses 8-9)

The Second Trumpet is sounded, and a great burning mountain (possibly an asteroid or volcano) is cast into the sea. One-third of the life in the sea and one-third of the ships are destroyed.

The Sounding of the Third Trumpet
(Verses 10-11)

The Third Trumpet is sounded, and a great star named Wormwood falls from heaven, burning like a lamp. When it lands, it poisons one-third of the fresh water. Many people die because of the poisoned water.

The Sounding of the Fourth Trumpet
(Verse 12)

The Fourth Trumpet is sounded, and a third of the light from the sun, moon, and stars is darkened, while a third of the light of the night and day is diminished.

- This clearly demonstrates God's control over the earth, the heavens, and the forces of nature (which pagan man has worshipped throughout the ages).
- This is only one of several instances of celestial phenomena that occur throughout the broad Day of the Lord.

Three Woes Are Coming
(Verse 13)

An eagle (some translations say an "angel") then declares that "Three Woes" are coming with the next three Trumpet Judgments, warning of the great suffering that is about to occur.

"Then I looked, and I heard an eagle crying with a loud voice as it flew directly overhead,. "Woe, woe, woe to those who dwell on the earth,

at the blasts of the other trumpets that the three angels are about to blow!"

-Revelation 8:13 (ESV)

The next three Trumpet Judgments are even more terrifying than those that preceded them. They involve the temporary release of the fallen angels that sinned with women in Genesis 6:1-4, who have since that time been bound in the bottomless pit, also called the abyss or Tartarus – the lowest part of hell (Cross-reference with Jude 1:6-7; 2 Peter 2:4-9; 1 Peter 3:18-20). Prior to their own final judgments, they are temporarily released in order to bring terror upon the earth at this time.

The Sounding of the Fifth Trumpet
(Chapter 9:1-12)

The Fifth Trumpet is sounded, and a star falls from heaven and is given the key to the bottomless pit (the abyss, or Tartarus). The sun and air are darkened as hordes of imprisoned fallen angels (appearing like warrior locusts) are released to torment the earth dwellers. They are led by a king called Apollyon, or Abaddon (meaning "the destroyer"). This is the First Woe!

- While many of the other judgments do involve actual celestial phenomena, the "star" that falls here seems to instead refer to a personage (Verse 1 refers to the star as "him"). This star would appear to be an angel that God tasks with opening the abyss in order to bring about the next stage of divine judgment.
- The king that emerges is called "the **angel** of the bottomless pit," which provides a strong clue that the "locusts" led by this king are also fallen angels.

- These "locusts" do not harm vegetation (like real locusts would), but instead inflict pain and torment upon all those who do not have the seal of God. People will desire to die because of the pain, but death will evade them.
- This torment will last for a period of five months – the identical time period that God's judgment lasted during the flood (Genesis 7:11, 24 and 8:3-4), which destroyed the antediluvian world that had become corrupted by the illicit activities of these fallen angels.
- The release of this army of "locusts" is also prophesied in Joel Chapter 2.
- Following this First Woe/Fifth Trumpet, two additional woes are yet to come.

"The first woe has passed; behold, two woes are still to come."
-Revelation 9:12 (ESV)

The Sounding of the Sixth Trumpet
(Verses 13-21)

The Sixth Trumpet is sounded and four imprisoned fallen angels are released from the river Euphrates. John sees an army of two hundred million horsemen who would kill a third of the population of the earth. This is the Second Woe!

- These angels have been bound there in preparation for being loosed at this exact time. They are released to lead this army of horsemen.
- The horsemen are described as having breastplates of fire, with smoke and brimstone issuing from their mouths. They are said to have power in their mouths and in their tails.

- Those that survive this Second Woe still refuse to repent of their murders, their sorceries, their sexual immorality, and their thefts.

The Interlude Between the Sixth and Seventh Trumpets – Chapters 10 to 11:13

At this point, we now encounter the second of the five parenthetical segments included within Revelation. The narrative pauses between the Sixth and Seventh Trumpets in order to provide explanatory information concerning other events relevant to this time.

The Mighty Angel and the Small Scroll
(Chapter 10)

A mighty angel with a small scroll stands with one foot on the land and one foot on the sea, and with a loud voice declares that time shall be no more. Then Seven Thunders utter their voices.

- John was about to write the message of the Thunders, but is instead told to seal up the message and not write it.
- He is told that the mystery of God is about to be finished.
- John is told to eat the small scroll; it was sweet to the taste but bitter to the stomach (similar to Ezekiel 3:1-3).

The Third Temple
(Chapter 11:1-2)

Chapter 11 begins by taking for granted that a Jewish temple will exist during this time period. This is one of the Biblical reasons that we expect the temple in Jerusalem (which doesn't exist at the time of this writing) to be rebuilt (that being the third temple).

- The first temple was built by Solomon. The second temple was built by Zerubbabel and was later enlarged by Herod. The third temple will be the one in existence during the Tribulation. After that, a fourth temple will be built by Jesus as the Millennial Kingdom begins.
- John was given a measuring rod to measure the (third) temple but was told not to measure the outer court, which was for the Gentiles. The Gentile nations would continue to oppress Israel for forty-two months (the last three and a half years of the Tribulation).

The Two Witnesses
(Chapter 11:3-13)

Two witnesses are mentioned, who will carry on a prophetic ministry during the Tribulation. By their description, it appears they will be Moses and Elijah, as both performed similar miraculous wonders to those detailed in Verse 6. Others believe they are Enoch and Elijah, since they will be the only two non-Church Age believers to have never died a natural death (both were "raptured").

- The Two Witnesses will prophesy for 1,260 days, or three and a half years. They will be given great power, and no one is able to hurt them. After their period of ministry is completed, the Beast will make war with them and be allowed to overcome them.

- When they are finally killed by the Antichrist, there will be a great celebration on the earth, and their bodies will lay in the street for three and a half days. After the three and a half days, God will resurrect them and call them to heaven. This call is similar to that seen in Chapter 4 when John was called up to heaven ("Come up here"). The world, which watches this take place, will be in utter amazement.
- A great earthquake will then destroy a tenth part of Jerusalem, and seven thousand people die. When this occurs, a remnant within the city gives glory to God.

This ends the second parenthetical segment of Revelation, as the narrative will now continue with the sounding of the Seventh Trumpet.

The Sounding of the Seventh Trumpet – Chapter 11:14-19

The Seventh Trumpet is sounded, and great voices in heaven declare that the kingdoms of this world have become the kingdoms of the Lord. Just as the Seventh Seal released the Seven Trumpet Judgments, the Seventh Trumpet will release the Seven Bowl Judgments, comprising the finality of God's wrath. This is the Third Woe!

- Jesus Christ's coming rule upon the earth is so certain that it is described here as though it were already starting. This is called a **proleptic** statement.
- The Twenty-Four Elders fall before the throne declaring the deity and power of Jesus Christ, and that the full wrath of God is about to be completed with the pouring of the Bowl Judgments.

- The temple doors in heaven are opened, and the Ark of God is revealed, representing God's covenant with Israel.

Notes

7

THE INTERLUDE BEFORE THE BOWLS
REVELATION CHAPTERS 12 TO 14

The Celestial Signs: The Woman, the Child, and the Dragon – Chapter 12

At this point, we now encounter the third of the five parenthetical segments included within Revelation. The narrative pauses between the Seventh Trumpet and the pouring of the Seven Bowls in order to provide explanatory information concerning other events relevant to this time.

John sees a great sign appear in heaven – a woman clothed with the sun, having the moon under her feet and wearing a crown of twelve stars. She was pregnant and cried out in labor as she was about to give birth.

He then sees another sign appear in heaven – a great, fiery red dragon with seven heads and ten horns, having seven crowns on its heads. Its tail swept away a third of the stars in heaven and hurled them to the earth. The Dragon stood in front of the Woman who was about to give birth, ready to devour her Child.

- The Woman clothed with the sun, having the moon under her feet and a crown of twelve stars on her head, represents Israel (Cross-reference with Genesis 37:9-11, in which Joseph's dream identifies these celestial symbols as referring to Jacob, his wife, and the twelve sons).
- Verse 9 identifies the Dragon as Satan, who swept a third part of the stars from heaven. The stars are the fallen angels that defected with him in his rebellion.
- The Child born from the Woman, who "was to rule all nations with a rod of iron" and "was caught up unto God, and to his throne," is clearly Jesus Christ (Cross-reference with Psalm 2:9; Revelation 2:27; 19:5).
- The Dragon, who is the accuser of the brethren, is cast down to the earth during the Day of the Lord. He is filled with wrath because he knows his time is short.
- The Dragon then makes war with the Woman (Israel), but God protects her. She escapes and is nourished in a wilderness location prepared by God. There she is protected for a duration of 1,260 days (the second half of the Tribulation, called the Great Tribulation by Jesus in Matthew 24:21).

The Rise of the Two Beasts – Chapter 13

John is now introduced to a new scene that further describes the Dragon's warfare against the saints. Understanding Daniel's visions in the book of Daniel will aid our understanding.

The First Beast
(Verses 1-10)

The First Beast rises out of the **sea**. This Beast has seven heads and ten horns, with diadems (or crowns) on each horn.

- Some have understood the sea to represent the Gentile nations. This seems to be supported by Revelation 17:15. The sea may also relate to the abyss, from which John says the Beast emerges (Revelation 11:7 and 17:8). The apostle Paul also equates the sea and the abyss in Romans 10:7, in which he cites Deuteronomy 30:13. Could it be that the entrance to the abyss is beneath the sea?
- The Beast's power is given to him by the Dragon (Satan).
- The Beast is described as a composite of the beasts Daniel saw in Daniel 7, where successive Gentile world empires are described as a lion (Babylon), a bear (Medo-Persia), and a leopard (Greece). The fourth empire (Rome) combines the three previous animal characteristics, and therefore is far more dreadful than each of the previous empires. John's vision mentions these animals in reverse order, showing how while Daniel was looking forward in time, John was looking back in time.
- This First Beast appears to represent a revived manifestation of the fourth empire (a revived Roman empire) that will rise during the Day of the Lord, since the description is similar to Daniel 7:7-8 and Revelation 12:3 and 17:3, 7. This Beast is not only representative of this empire as a whole, but also, in a more specific sense, the leader of the empire – the Antichrist (Cross-reference Revelation 13:8 with 17:8).
- The Beast's ten horns seem to refer to the ten kings/kingdoms that give their power to the Beast

during the final world empire (Cross-reference with Revelation 17:12, 18). Three of the ten are overthrown by the Beast (the "little horn" of Daniel 7:8), yielding a remnant of seven, which some have associated with the seven heads. Another possibility is that the seven heads represent the seven successive Gentile world empires that may also be alluded to later in Revelation 17:9-11 (likely Egypt, Assyria, Babylon, Medo-Persia, Greece, Rome, and the final world empire).

- One of the Beast's heads is mortally wounded but is revived to life. This revived head wound seems to represent the Antichrist as the head and personification of this final world empire. This healing causes the earth dwellers to worship the Dragon, who gave his power to the Beast.

- The Beast blasphemes God and makes war with the saints and persecutes them (those converted to Christ during the Day of the Lord, likely through the witness of the 144,000 and the Two Witnesses).

- The Beast is allowed to exercise authority for forty-two months, which seems to refer to the final half of the Tribulation (the Great Tribulation, or the last three and a half years of the final seven-year "week").

The Second Beast
(Verses 11-18)

The Second Beast rises from the **earth**, exercising religious and civil power. This Beast is the False Prophet who has horns as a lamb but speaks as a dragon, and whose actions support the activities of the First Beast.

- This Second Beast is said to come out of the earth, rather than the sea. Those who believe the sea refers to the Gentile nations normally then take the earth to mean Israel.
- This Beast seems to act as the primary "assistant" of the First Beast by implementing His agenda.
- The "horns like a lamb" suggest a deceptive appearance of harmlessness. However, when he speaks, he is communicating through the Dragon's power.
- This Beast displays great power and performs great signs such as calling fire down from the heavens. These counterfeit signs aid in the deception of the earth dwellers, leading them to create and then worship an image of the First Beast. He causes the image to live and speak, furthering the deception.
- The whole earth is forced to take the number of the Beast (666, which is the number of his name) on their forehead or right hand. No one can buy or sell without the mark. Those who refuse to take the mark are killed.

The Redeemed and the Angels' Messages – Chapter 14:1-13

The 144,000 Jewish Evangelists
(Verses 1-5)

The scene opens with the Lamb standing on Mt. Zion in heaven with the 144,000 Jewish evangelists who had the Father's name written in their foreheads. The 144,000 are before the Twenty-Four Elders in heaven, singing a new song that only they can sing. They are pure and holy, and they follow the Lamb wherever He goes.

The Proclamations of the Three Angels
(Verses 6-13)

John sees three angels in succession flying over the earth, each with a different message. Those who heed the messages will be blessed.

- The first angel proclaims the everlasting gospel.
- The second angel proleptically declares "Babylon has fallen," indicating the coming destruction of the false religious system and empire of the Beast.
- The third angel proclaims judgment on all those who take the mark of the Beast.

The Harvest is Ripe and the Reaping Begins – Chapter 14:14-20

- The scene opens with the Son of Man sitting on a white cloud wearing a golden crown and holding a sharp sickle.
- An angel declares that the time has come to harvest the earth – a proclamation of the coming final judgment.
- Another angel appears with a sharp sickle and joins the harvest.
- Then another angel appears, having power over fire. He instructs the angel with the sickle to reap the harvest of the earth.
- Verse 20 points to the Battle of Armageddon, with more detail to be revealed in Chapter 19.
- "Without the city" means outside of Jerusalem. In the Old Testament, the prophets foretold that the final battle would occur outside of Jerusalem in the Valley

of Jehoshaphat, which is traditionally located in the area of the Kidron Valley (Joel 3:12-14; Zechariah 14:4).

- It has been suggested that Armageddon (which is not near Jerusalem) is not the actual location of the battle but is rather the staging grounds for the battle that will take place near Jerusalem. Another possibility is that the battle is so widespread it will reach from outside Jerusalem all the way to the area of Armageddon (the Valley of Megiddo).

- The blood will flow to the height of a horse's bridle for a distance of about 180 miles. This is about the distance from Bozrah in the southeast to Megiddo in the north.

- Cross-reference this "stomping of the winepress" with Isaiah 63, where the returning Messiah is pictured as approaching Jerusalem from Bozrah after trodding the winepress of His fury. Bozrah, in southwest Jordan, is the location of the wilderness cave city of Petra, to which many believe the Woman (the remnant of Israel) will escape the persecution of the Dragon during the Great Tribulation.

This ends the third parenthetical segment of Revelation, as the narrative will now continue with the pouring of the Seven Bowls.

Notes

8

THE POURING OF THE SEVEN BOWLS
REVELATION CHAPTERS 15 TO 16

Preparation For the Bowl Judgments – Chapter 15

"Then I saw another sign in heaven, great and amazing, seven angels with seven plagues, which are the last, for with them the wrath of God is finished."
  -Revelation 15:1 (ESV)

- Those who had gotten victory over the Beast, his image, and his mark are seen in heaven holding harps and singing the song of Moses. These are the Tribulation saints who responded to the gospel that was proclaimed by the 144,000, the Two Witnesses, and the angel who encircled the earth preaching (Revelation 14:6).
- The temple in heaven opens, and the seven angels are given seven vials (or bowls). These final Bowl Judgments act as the "grand finale" of God's wrath.

- The temple was filled with smoke and the glory of God such that none were able to enter until these last plagues had been poured out.

The Seven Bowls Are Poured Out – Chapter 16

"Then I heard a loud voice from the temple telling the seven angels, 'Go and pour out on the earth the seven bowls of the wrath of God.'"
-Revelation 16:1 (ESV)

The Pouring of the First Bowl
(Verse 2)

The First Bowl is poured out, and horrible, malignant sores break out on everyone who has the mark of the Beast and who worships his image.

The Pouring of the Second Bowl
(Verse 3)

The Second Bowl is poured out on the sea, and it becomes like the blood of a corpse. Everything in the sea dies.

The Pouring of the Third Bowl
(Verses 4-7)

The Third Bowl is poured out on the rivers and springs, and they become blood. An angel declares that this judgment of blood is because they had shed the innocent blood of the saints and prophets.

The Pouring of the Fourth Bowl
(Verses 8-9)

The Fourth Bowl is poured out and the sun scorches the earth dwellers with fire and intense heat. They blaspheme the name of God and do not repent nor give Him glory.

The Pouring of the Fifth Bowl
(Verses 10-11)

The Fifth Bowl is poured out, and the throne of the Beast and his kingdom are plunged into darkness. The earth dwellers grind their teeth in anguish, cursing God for their pains and sores. They still do not repent of their evil deeds nor turn to God.

The Pouring of the Sixth Bowl
(Verse 12)

The Sixth Bowl is poured out, and the great Euphrates River is dried up, allowing the kings of the east to march their armies west.

The Interlude Between the Sixth and Seventh Bowls
(Verses 13-16)

At this point, we now encounter the fourth of the five parenthetical segments included within Revelation. The narrative briefly pauses between the Sixth and Seventh Bowls in order to provide further information concerning all that is taking place.

- Three unclean spirits resembling frogs come from the Dragon's mouth, from the Beast's mouth, and from the mouth of the False Prophet. They are demonic spirits performing signs, who go throughout the earth gathering the kings of the world for the final battle against God.

- They gather for battle at Armageddon (Megiddo, in the Jezreel Valley in northern Israel). This was a renowned battlefield of the ancient world. Armies from the east would have to cross the Euphrates River to get there, as is indicated in Verse 12.
- Jesus recapitulates a final warning to all Church Age readers regarding His imminent Parousia ("coming"). Whoever is not ready will be left to face the broad period of the Day of the Lord and its sequence of judgments (that began in Chapter 6). Now nearing its climax, Jesus reissues this warning.

This ends the fourth parenthetical segment of Revelation, as the narrative will now continue with the pouring of the Seventh Bowl.

The Pouring of the Seventh Bowl
(Verses 17-21)

The Seventh Bowl is poured out, and a voice from the throne of God declares, "It is done!" Lightning and thunder break out, and the greatest earthquake in human history takes place.

- The earthquake causes "the great city" to split into three parts. This is a clear reference to Jerusalem (Cross-reference with Revelation 11:8, which identifies Jerusalem with this same title). Many Gentile cities are destroyed, and Babylon the Great (the headquarters of the Beast) falls. The earthquake is so great that it displaces islands and mountains.
- Great hailstones weighing around one hundred pounds each fall from heaven and pummel the earth. Still, the surviving earth dwellers curse God.

Notes

9

THE FALL OF RELIGIOUS BABYLON

REVELATION CHAPTER 17

The Harlot Who Rides the Beast – Chapter 17:1-6a

At this point, we now encounter the fifth of the five parenthetical segments included within Revelation. The narrative pauses between the Seventh Bowl and the Second Coming proper in order to provide explanatory information concerning the fall of Babylon and the subsequent rejoicing in heaven. The chronological sequence then resumes in Revelation 19:11.

This chapter and the next detail the final destruction of Babylon in its religious and political/commercial forms. After describing the Seven Bowl Judgments in the previous chapter, the narrative now pauses to insert a deeper explanation of the city's destruction. Chapter 17 deals with the religious aspect and Chapter 18 concerns the political/commercial aspect.

"Then one of the seven angels who had the seven bowls came and said to me, 'Come, I will show you the judgment of the great prostitute who is seated on many waters, with whom the kings of the earth have committed sexual immorality, and with the wine of whose sexual immorality the dwellers on earth have become drunk.'"

-Revelation 17:1-2 (ESV)

John is then carried away into the wilderness and shown the judgment of a harlot (or prostitute) who sat upon a scarlet-colored beast that had seven heads, ten horns, and bore blasphemous names.

- The Harlot is dressed in purple and scarlet, representing spiritual fornication, false religion, and false worship. She holds a golden cup full of the filth of her immorality.
- She represents the pagan false religious system of the earth that goes back to the Tower of Babel and has woven itself through history ever since. Babylon in scripture becomes a label for these false religious systems that pervade history.
- On her forehead was written a name: "Mystery, Babylon the great, mother of prostitutes and of earth's abominations."
- She is described as drunk on the blood of the saints, referring to the continual persecution of God's people by the apostate religious system down through time.
- The woman's position on top of the beast (or riding the beast) depicts the initial influence of the apostate world religious system over the political system of the Beast in the end-times. The scarlet beast she rides is the same Beast who emerged out of the sea in Revelation 13:1 (the First Beast).

The Significance of the Symbolism – Chapter 17:6b-18

> *"When I saw her, I marveled greatly. But the angel said to me, 'Why do you marvel? I will tell you the mystery of the woman, and of the beast with seven heads and ten horns that carries her.'"*
> -Revelation 17:6b-7 (ESV)

When John saw this great sight, he was amazed and wondered after it. Seeing this, the angel begins to give him understanding as to the meaning of the symbolism.

First, the angel reveals the identity of the Beast by using several details from Chapters 11 and 13, to which he also adds new information.

> *"The beast that you saw **was, and is not, and is about to rise from the bottomless pit and go to destruction.** And the dwellers on earth whose names have not been written in the book of life from the foundation of the world will marvel to see the beast, **because it was and is not and is to come."***
> -Revelation 17:8 (ESV)

- This description of "was, is not, and is to come" seems to identify him as the Beast from Chapter 13 that was healed of a mortal head wound (Revelation 13:3-4).
- "Is not" in Verse 8 seems to prophetically refer to the Beast's death. Since this is a prophetic statement, it seems best to place the "is not" condition of the Beast completely in the future.
- His rise from the bottomless pit seems to refer to his resurrection ("is to come"), which connects with Revelation 13:14 and 17:11.

The angel then continues to reveal the identity of the Beast.

"This calls for a mind with wisdom: **the seven heads are seven mountains** *on which the woman is seated;* **they are also seven kings,** *five of whom have fallen, one is, the other has not yet come, and when he does come he must remain only a little while. As for the beast that was and is not, it is* **an eighth but it belongs to the seven,** *and it goes to destruction."*

-Revelation 17:9-11 (ESV)

- The seven heads = seven mountains = seven kings = seven kingdoms. This symbolism appears to describe seven consecutive Gentile world rulers and/or empires. In other words, it describes seven empires with seven kings who each act as a personification of their empire. In Daniel 7:17 and 23, we see that kings and kingdoms are often used interchangeably.
- Five have fallen, one is (meaning at the time John saw the vision), and one is to come (which is the Antichrist), and he will receive power for a short time.
- How can we consider the "is not" reference point in Verse 8 as being **future**, while at the same time consider this sixth kingdom that "is" to refer to John's **present** day at the time he received the vision? The answer is that Verse 8 was entirely prophetic, whereas the explanation given in Verses 9-11 was inserted to help make the prophecy understandable.

These seven mountains/kings/kingdoms likely represent the seven Gentile kingdoms that have dominated the world scene and oppressed the nation of Israel throughout history:

1.) Egypt (fallen)
2.) Assyria (fallen)

3.) Babylon (fallen)
4.) Medo-Persia (fallen)
5.) Greece (fallen)
6.) Rome (is)
7.) The future kingdom of the Beast (is to come)

- Mysteriously, the Beast is said to be one of the seven heads, but at the same time is also the eighth head. This is likely related to the fatal head wound that the Beast receives. We are told that he resurrects, which causes the world to marvel and follow after him. This would seem to represent his reappearance as the eighth king.
- When he begins his political career, he is human (the seventh head). But when he returns, he is superhuman, or even Satan incarnate (the eighth head).
- As the Antichrist, the Beast is the ultimate false Messiah. Like Jesus resurrected, the Beast will also be resurrected. Whether this is an actual resurrection or just deception, it may clarify the mystery of the Beast as being both the seventh and the eighth heads.

*"And **the ten horns that you saw are ten kings** who have not yet received royal power, but they are to receive authority as kings for one hour, together with the beast. These are of one mind, and they hand over their power and authority to the beast."*
-Revelation 17:12-13 (ESV)

- John is told that the Beast's ten horns represent ten kings who join in a confederacy under the Beast in the final world kingdom.

*"And the ten horns that you saw, they and the beast will hate the prosti-
tute. They will make her desolate and naked, and devour her flesh and
burn her up with fire, for God has put it into their hearts to carry out his
purpose by being of one mind and handing over their royal power to the
beast, until the words of God are fulfilled. And the woman that you saw
is the great city that has dominion over the kings of the earth."*

-Revelation 17:16-18 (ESV)

- The Harlot sits on many waters. Verse 15 identifies
  this symbolism as referring to the peoples and nations
  and languages that she controls.
- The Antichrist will initially use the Harlot (the false
  religious system) to consolidate his power – even
  appearing subservient to her, as she is pictured riding
  him – but will then destroy her so that he alone will
  be worshiped.
- The Harlot is destroyed by the Beast and his ten-
  kingdom confederacy, which helps us recognize the
  Harlot's identity as religious Babylon, and that her
  destruction probably occurs as the Beast attempts to
  set himself up as God.
- The Beast will destroy religious Babylon (the Harlot)
  in favor of a deified political dictator (the Beast from
  the sea in Chapter 13).

Notes

10

THE FALL OF
POLITICAL/COMMERCIAL BABYLON
REVELATION CHAPTERS 18 TO 19:5

Babylon Is Fallen – Chapter 18

Chapter 18 continues the parenthetical insertion that began in Chapter 17 and portrays the fall of the political and economic aspect of Babylon.

What does Revelation mean when it refers to Babylon here? Many identify Babylon as referring to Rome, while others believe that the actual geographical city of Babylon on the Euphrates River will in some way be rebuilt in the end-times. If the more literal view is embraced, then Babylon must again rise to prominence in order for its final destruction to occur, as is prophesied here (Cross-reference with Isaiah 13 and Jeremiah 51, which also describe a final judgment for Babylon that appears to currently remain unfulfilled).

- The city will be the center for both false religion and economic prosperity during the end-times. It will act as the focal point for the Beast's system that will oppose and persecute God's people.

- The religious system associated with the city will thrive for a period of time until the Beast and his ten-kingdom confederacy no longer have need of it (the destruction discussed in the previous chapter).
- After the fall of its religious aspect, the city will continue to act as the headquarters of the Beast's final world empire until its ultimate destruction (depicted here in Chapter 18).

"After this I saw another angel coming down from heaven, having great authority, and the earth was made bright with his glory. And he called out with a mighty voice, 'Fallen, fallen is Babylon the great!'"
-Revelation 18:1-2 (ESV)

- An angel lights up the whole earth and declares the fall of Babylon.
- The city, which is the center of this global system, is destroyed and becomes the habitation of every kind of evil spirit (Cross-reference with Isaiah 13:21-22).
- The kings and nations will mourn, because through her they received great wealth.
- The cry to "come out of her my people" is applicable for all of God's people throughout the ages.
- A mighty angel declares that Babylon will be found no more.

Rejoicing in Heaven – Chapter 19:1-5

"After this I heard what seemed to be the loud voice of a great multitude in heaven, crying out, 'Hallelujah! Salvation and glory and power belong to our God, for his judgments are true and just; for he has judged the great prostitute who corrupted the earth with her immorality, and has avenged on her the blood of his servants.'"

-Revelation 19:1-2 (ESV)

- Following the final destruction of both religious and commercial Babylon, there is great rejoicing heard in heaven.
- A voice that sounds like a multitude praises God for avenging the blood of His people that Babylon had spilled.
- This rejoicing seems to take place directly prior to Christ's Second Coming proper.
- The Twenty-Four Elders and the Four Living Creatures then fall down in worship before the throne of God.
- Another voice is then heard from the throne, calling for all of God's servants to praise Him.

Notes

11

THE MARRIAGE SUPPER OF THE LAMB AND THE SECOND COMING
REVELATION CHAPTER 19:6-21

The Announcement of the Marriage Supper of the Lamb – Chapter 19:6-10

As Chapter 19 begins, the parenthetical segment that began back in Chapter 17 continues as an expansion of the events connected to the Seventh Bowl Judgment.

As all of heaven rejoices and praises God for the destruction of Babylon in all of its forms, the praise then transitions to the celebration of the coming Marriage Supper of the Lamb.

*"Then I heard what seemed to be the voice of a great multitude, like the roar of many waters and like the sound of mighty peals of thunder, crying out, 'Hallelujah! For the Lord our God the Almighty reigns. Let us rejoice and exult and give him the glory, for **the marriage of the Lamb has come, and his Bride has made herself ready**; it was granted her to clothe herself with fine linen, bright and pure' – for the fine linen is the righteous deeds of the saints. And the angel said to me, 'Write this: Blessed are those who are invited to **the marriage supper of the Lamb.'** And he said to me, 'These are the true words of God.'"*
-Revelation 19:6-9 (ESV)

- Notice that Verse 7 first mentions the marriage and Verse 9 then mentions the supper. Many see these as being the same event, while others see them as two separate events happening at different times and in different locations.
- Those who believe they are the same event generally see it as taking place in heaven prior to the Second Coming proper. Meanwhile, those who believe them to be separate events see the marriage taking place in heaven prior to the Second Coming proper, but the supper taking place on earth after the Second Coming proper, as the Millennium begins (Cross-reference with Isaiah 25:6; Matthew 8:11; 26:29; Luke 13:28-29; 22:16-18, 29-30).
- The Lamb's Bride is the Church, which had been raptured prior to the beginning of the Day of the Lord and all of its judgments. Old Testament saints and Tribulation saints are not part of the Bride of Christ. Notice the distinction in Verse 9 between the Bride and those who are invited as guests to the supper. Throughout the New Testament, the Church alone is clearly described as being the Bride (Romans 7:1-4; Ephesians 5:31-32; 2 Corinthians 11:2).

The typology of the Hebrew wedding is important to understand here. Ancient Hebrew weddings included three major aspects:

1. A marriage contract with suitable bride price (or down payment) paid by the bridegroom
2. The catching away of the bride, in which the bride would be escorted from her house to the home of the bridegroom's father

3. The marriage celebration that followed, which included a great feast (or supper)

This perfectly corresponds to the Biblical portrayal of the Church as the Bride of Christ:

1. Christ redeemed (or purchased) us, with His sinless blood being the bride price (Ephesians 1:14; 1 Peter 1:18-19; 1 Corinthians 6:19-20).
2. Those who have been redeemed will be caught up by the Bridegroom Christ in the Rapture and escorted to His Father's house in heaven, where there is a place prepared for us (John 14:1-3).
3. We will then participate in the great Marriage Supper of the Lamb.

This ends the fifth parenthetical segment of Revelation, as the focus will now shift back to the earth as the narrative continues with Christ's Second Coming proper.

The Second Coming – Chapter 19:11-21

After the announcement of the Marriage Supper, John sees the heavens open and the Lord Jesus coming out on a white horse!

> "Then I saw heaven opened, and behold, a white horse! **The one sitting on it is called Faithful and True**, and in righteousness he judges and makes war. His eyes are like a flame of fire, and on his head are many diadems, and he has a name written that no one knows but himself. **He is clothed in a robe dipped in blood, and the name by which he is called is The Word of God.** And the armies of heaven, arrayed in fine linen, white and pure, were following him on white horses."
> -Revelation 19:11-14 (ESV)

- Unlike the previous rider on the white horse (the Antichrist, who came forth at the opening of the First Seal), this rider is described as being faithful and true. The world's pseudo-ruler (the Antichrist) is replaced with the true and rightful ruler who alone was worthy to open the seven-sealed scroll and reclaim the title deed for the whole earth (Revelation 5).

- A white horse is a symbol of triumph. Jesus is returning to triumph over His enemies, bring divine judgment, and establish His righteous rule on the earth (a thousand-year period to follow called the Millennial Kingdom).

- At His First Coming, He came as a lamb, but at His Second Coming, He will come as a lion. At His First Coming, He was the suffering Servant, but at His Second Coming, He will be the conquering King. The Jews expected a king messiah first, but Jesus's priority at that time was His mission of redemption. The King would not come until redemption was first purchased!

- He is called faithful and true, for one thing, because in order to keep His covenants with Israel, He must return to save the Jewish remnant that had turned to Him in faith during the Tribulation. He is faithful and true to His unconditional covenant promises! In Matthew 24:22, Jesus told us that if He didn't return, no flesh would be saved. In other words, if this time period of Tribulation was allowed to continue past its allotted time, all people on earth – and certainly the Jewish remnant – would be destroyed. If there is no Jewish remnant remaining, then God couldn't fulfill His covenant promises to Israel, and the Millennial Kingdom (which is all about Israel) could not take place. In order to fulfill His promises, His glorious Second Coming proper is necessary.

- Jesus's Second Coming proper is the climax of the final seven-year period and can be considered the climactic event of human history. This comprises the **narrow** sense of the Day of the Lord. Both the Old and New Testaments foretell this event with great clarity (Cross-reference with Zechariah 14:3-4; Matthew 24:27-31).

- He is described as wearing a robe dipped in blood, which in this case seems to refer to the blood of His enemies. It is proleptic, as is His white horse and crown. In other words, it looks forward to His certain victory that would follow (Cross-reference with Isaiah 63:1-6).

- The armies of heaven follow Christ on white horses, clothed in white, clean linen. These are the redeemed saints of God returning with Him.

*"From his mouth comes a sharp sword with which **to strike down the nations, and he will rule them with a rod of iron**. He will tread the winepress of the fury of the wrath of God the Almighty. On his robe and on his thigh he has a name written, King of kings and Lord of lords."*
-Revelation 19:15-16 (ESV)

- Jesus will smite the wicked nations and bring the entire earth under His righteous rule. He will establish His Millennial Kingdom and rule justly with a "rod of iron" (Cross-reference with Psalm 2:9; Revelation 2:27).

- Jesus wears the title "King of kings and Lord of lords," demonstrating His power, majesty, and rightful rule over the earth.

The Other Supper: The Defeat of the Beast and His Army – Chapter 19:17-21

"Then I saw an angel standing in the sun, and with a loud voice he called to all the birds that fly directly overhead, "Come, gather for the great supper of God, to eat the flesh of kings, the flesh of captains, the flesh of mighty men, the flesh of horses and their riders, and the flesh of all men, both free and slave, both small and great."
-Revelation 19:17-18 (ESV)

- The two Beasts (the Antichrist and the False Prophet) are taken and cast alive into the Lake of Fire.
- All those who have the mark of the Beast and all the army of the Antichrist are destroyed by the power of Jesus Christ.
- The birds of the earth feast on the carnage. Which of the two suppers would you like to attend?

Notes

12

THE MILLENNIAL KINGDOM
REVELATION CHAPTER 20

Satan Is Bound – Chapter 20:1-3

"Then I saw an angel coming down from heaven, holding in his hand the key to the bottomless pit and a great chain. And he seized the dragon, that ancient serpent, who is the devil and Satan, and bound him for a thousand years, and threw him into the pit, and shut it and sealed it over him, so that he might not deceive the nations any longer, until the thousand years were ended. After that he must be released for a little while."
 -Revelation 20:1-3 (ESV)

- An angel with the key to the bottomless pit binds Satan with a great chain and casts him into the abyss for a thousand years (the duration of the Millennial Kingdom).
- The phrase "a thousand years" occurs six times throughout Chapter 20. The English word "millennium" comes from the Latin *mille annum*, which means "a thousand years." **Premillennialists** understand this to mean a literal future thousand

years, during which Christ will physically reign upon the earth from Jerusalem. This Millennium, or Millennial Kingdom will be a fulfillment of the many Old Testament prophecies concerning an earthly reign of Christ. During this time, the earth is partially restored, the knowledge of God is widespread, sin is immediately judged, and a restored Israel is the predominant nation on the earth. On the other hand, **Amillenialists** believe that this Kingdom is being fulfilled today. They do not believe in a literal future thousand-year reign of Christ. Instead, they interpret it allegorically as a figurative picture of the present Church Age. As Premillennial commentators often note, if we're living in the Kingdom right now, then Satan's chain is a bit too loose!

- After the thousand years, Satan is released for a short time and will be allowed to temporarily deceive the nations one final time.

The Earthly Kingdom Reign of Christ – Chapter 20:4-6

*"Then I saw thrones, and seated on them were those to whom the authority to judge was committed. Also I saw the souls of those who had been beheaded for the testimony of Jesus and for the word of God, and those who had not worshiped the beast or its image and had not received its mark on their foreheads or their hands. They came to life and reigned with Christ for a thousand years. The rest of the dead did not come to life until the thousand years were ended. **This is the first resurrection.** Blessed and holy is the one who shares in the first resurrection! Over such the second death has no power, but they will be priests of God and of Christ, and they will reign with him for a thousand years."*

-Revelation 20:4-6 (ESV)

- John sees certain ones sitting on thrones with the power to issue judgment. These figures can probably be identified as the Church, who is said to reign on earth with Christ during the Millennium, judging the world (Cross-reference with 1 Corinthians 6:1-3; 2 Timothy 2:11-12; Revelation 2:26; 3:21; 5:9-10). Old Testament saints may also be included. In addition, the passage explicitly states that the resurrected Tribulation martyrs will also reign with Christ in the Kingdom.

- There is often confusion concerning the end of Verse 4 and how it relates to the two parts of Verse 5. Verse 4 describes the resurrection of the martyred Tribulation saints. The beginning of Verse 5 ("The rest of the dead did not come to life until the thousand years were ended") is parenthetical. The next sentence ("This is the first resurrection") connects to the end of Verse 4 (the resurrection of the martyred Tribulation saints).

- The First Resurrection is a multi-phased event that began with Jesus's resurrection along with a handful of Old Testament saints (1 Corinthians 15:20; Matthew 27:52-53), and includes the subsequent resurrection of the Church Age believers at the Rapture (1 Thessalonians 4:16-17), the Old Testament saints at the end of the Tribulation (Daniel 12:1-2), and concludes with the resurrection of the martyred Tribulation saints at the beginning of the Millennial Kingdom (Revelation 20:4-5).

- After the Tribulation martyrs are resurrected, the remaining dead (the wicked dead) are not raised and judged until the end of the Millennium (the Second Resurrection/Second Death – Verse 6).

- A blessing is pronounced upon those who take part in the First Resurrection, as it is the resurrection of life and blessing. The Second Resurrection is also called the Second Death because it is a resurrection of the wicked unto eternal damnation.

After the Thousand Years – Chapter 20:7-15

"And when the thousand years are expired, Satan shall be loosed out of his prison, and shall go out to deceive the nations which are in the four quarters of the earth, Gog, and Magog, to gather them together to battle: the number of whom is as the sand of the sea."
-Revelation 20:7-8 (KJV)

- At the end of the Millennium, Satan is loosed for a short period and goes out to deceive the nations one final time. A lesson from this is that even after a thousand years of peace with Jesus ruling justly on the earth, the sinful heart of mortal men will still rebel and follow after Satan. The problem is not our environment. The problem is the sin nature inside us that needs spiritual regeneration.
- Satan gathers a great army to the battle of Gog and Magog (different from the battle of the same name mentioned in Ezekiel 38, though it is likely named after it).
- The city of Jerusalem, home to the throne of Jesus Christ throughout the thousand years, is surrounded.
- Fire immediately comes down from heaven and destroys the armies. The Devil (Satan) is permanently cast into the Lake of Fire where the Beast and the False Prophet have been since the end of the Tribulation.

- After this comes the White Throne Judgment.
- Heaven and earth flee away from the presence of the One on the throne, who is Jesus.
- The rest of the dead (the wicked), both small and great, stand before the throne, and the books containing accounts of their deeds are opened. The Book of Life is also opened, and the wicked are judged by what is written in these books.
- Death and Hell, and those not found in the Book of Life are cast permanently into the Lake of Fire. This is the Second Death.

Notes

13

THE ETERNAL STATE

REVELATION CHAPTERS 21 TO 22

The New Heaven and New Earth – Chapter 21:1-8

"Then I saw a new heaven and a new earth, for the first heaven and the first earth had passed away, and the sea was no more. And I saw the holy city, new Jerusalem, coming down out of heaven from God, prepared as a bride adorned for her husband."
-Revelation 21:1-2 (ESV)

- Following the end of the Millennial Kingdom and White Throne Judgment, John's attention is now turned to the new heaven and new earth that will replace the old. Some believe this is an entirely new creation, while others believe it to be a renovation of the current heaven and earth.
- While today the waters cover most of the earth's surface, the new earth will apparently have no large bodies of water.
- John sees the city of God, the New Jerusalem, descending from heaven toward the earth. The city is

described as being adorned like a bride, since this city is the eternal home of the Bride.

- At this time, all of the effects of sin will be over. There will be no more death, no more pain, and no more suffering. All things will have become new!
- God will dwell eternally with His people in this city.

The New Jerusalem – Chapter 21:9-27

"Then came one of the seven angels who had the seven bowls full of the seven last plagues and spoke to me, saying, 'Come, I will show you the Bride, the wife of the Lamb.' And he carried me away in the Spirit to a great, high mountain, and showed me **the holy city Jerusalem coming down out of heaven from God,** *having the glory of God, its radiance like a most rare jewel, like a jasper, clear as crystal."*
-Revelation 21:9-11 (ESV)

- One of the angels offers John a more in-depth description of the holy city, New Jerusalem.
- Notice that the angel offered to show the Bride to John, and then showed him the city. Again, this is due to the fact that the city is the home of the Bride. If one wants to be shown the president, you might offer to take him to the White House. The White House is not the president, but it is where the president lives. This is why the angel showed John the city after offering to show him the Bride. The New Jerusalem is the eternal dwelling place of the Lord and His Bride.
- The believers of all ages will live in this city. It is the "city not built with hands" that Abraham yearned to see (Hebrews 11:10).
- The city is described as having a high wall with twelve gates and twelve angels. The names of the twelve sons

of Jacob (the tribes of Israel) are written, one on each gate.

- The city also has twelve foundations with one of the names of the twelve apostles written on each.
- An angel with a measuring rod measured the city and found its length, width, and height to each be 12,000 *stadia* (an ancient unit of measure). This would be equivalent to about 1,342 miles in each direction. Based on this description, the city is probably shaped as a cube, but could possibly even be a pyramid. The size of the city, if overlaid on top of the United States, would cover about half of the country! It would also extend upward past where the International Space Station is currently situated in low earth orbit!
- The wall of the city was measured to be 144 cubits high, which would be equivalent to over 200 feet. It is said to be made of jasper, a semiprecious stone that is usually reddish-brown in color.
- The city is pictured as descending from heaven and seems to imply that it will come to rest upon the earth. Some have speculated that it may hover over the earth (suspended as a satellite) during the Millennium, but then descend to rest upon the earth during the Eternal State.
- The city is described as appearing like clear glass with a golden cast to it. The foundation of the city is made up of multiple layers of gemstones: jasper, sapphire, agate, emerald, onyx, carnelian, chrysolite, beryl, topaz, chrysoprase, jacinth, and amethyst. Built into the walls are the twelve gates, which are each made up of one huge pearl. The streets of the city appear as gold but are transparent as glass.

- There is no temple in the city because God and the Lamb are the temple. There is also no sun or moon since the glory of God illuminates it.
- Nothing unclean will enter into this eternal city.

The River of Life – Chapter 22:1-5

*"Then the angel showed me **the river of the water of life, bright as crystal, flowing from the throne of God and of the Lamb** through the middle of the street of the city; also, on either side of the river, the tree of life with its twelve kinds of fruit, yielding its fruit each month. The leaves of the tree were for the healing of the nations."*
-Revelation 22:1-2 (ESV)

- John is then shown the River of Life that flows from the throne of God and through the middle of the city.
- On either side of the river is a Tree of Life, bearing twelve kinds of fruit (one for each month). Interestingly, this shows that although the Eternal State takes place outside of time as we know it, there will still be some way in which the passing of time or the seasons will be measured.
- The leaves of the trees are said to be for the healing of the nations, which seems to refer to the idea of serving or ministering to the nations. The leaves promote enjoyment of life in the New Jerusalem, not the correcting of sickness or ills (since there will be no more curse, nor its effects, as is stated in Verse 3).
- At this point, the curse will be completely gone. During the Millennium, the curse was partially lifted, but during the Eternal State it will be completely gone.

- The inhabitants of the city will enjoy immediate access to God, as He will dwell there with His people forever.

The Closing Words of the Book – Chapter 22:6-21

*"And he said to me, 'These words are trustworthy and true. And the Lord, the God of the spirits of the prophets, has sent his angel to show his servants **what must soon take place**. And behold, **I am coming soon**. Blessed is the one who keeps the words of the prophecy of this book.'"*
-Revelation 22:6-7 (ESV)

- The angel confirms the certainty of what was shown to John, describing this series of end-time events as coming "soon." This is a reference to the **imminence** of the beginning of this entire period (the broad Day of the Lord, whose opening event is the Rapture). It means that it can come to pass at any moment without preconditions. John and the Church of the first century were intended to expect the consummation of the age as being impending in their day, and we should have that same expectation today. This is then reemphasized in Jesus's statement that followed: "And behold, I am coming **soon**." The word "soon" again refers to imminence. It is an any-moment possibility.
- The imminence of this period is again confirmed in Verse 10 when the angel says to John, "Do not seal up the words of the prophecy of this book, for the time is **near** ...", and in Verse 12 when Jesus's warning is repeated ("Behold, I am coming **soon** ...").
- Clearly, the message to the reader is the need for spiritual readiness concerning His impending arrival.

One who is **spiritually prepared** to meet Jesus will be raptured and will then experience all of the blessings of the Marriage Supper, Millennial Kingdom, and Eternal State. One who is **spiritually unprepared** will be thrust into the Day of the Lord and will experience the judgments described throughout Revelation.

As the final chapter closes, Jesus issues several final statements concerning His identity.

> *"I am the Alpha and the Omega, the first and the last, the beginning and the end.'"*
> -Revelation 22:13 (ESV)

> *"I, Jesus, have sent my angel to testify to you about these things for the churches. I am the root and the descendant of David, the bright morning star."*
> -Revelation 22:16 (ESV)

- Keep in mind the first words of the book: "The revelation of Jesus Christ ..." (Revelation 1:1). We must remember that while it certainly does reveal events to come, a primary purpose of the book is to reveal the true identity and deity of Jesus Christ as the One God on the throne. It makes sense then, that as the book comes to a close, these revelations are reinforced.

As the book closes, it offers an invitation to the reader to take advantage of the salvation provided by its true Author.

> *"The Spirit and the Bride say, 'Come.' And let the one who hears say, 'Come.' And let the one who is thirsty come; let the one who desires take the water of life without price."*

-Revelation 22:17 (ESV)

- Here, we find an open invitation to all to receive and participate in the new life that Jesus Christ made available through His death, burial, and resurrection.
- This is the gospel invitation of the book of Revelation. It reflects a similar prophetic invitation found in Isaiah 55:1.

"Come, everyone who thirsts, come to the waters; and he who has no money, come, buy and eat! Come, buy wine and milk without money and without price."
-Isaiah 55:1 (ESV)

Today is the day to ensure you are on the right side of the supernatural conflict! Today is the day of grace! Today is the day to make your decision to follow Jesus and obey His gospel (Acts 2:38; 1 Corinthians 15:1-8; 2 Thessalonians 1:8; 1 Peter 4:17)!

Revelation ends with a final admonition and warning, again reinforcing the imminence of this coming period.

"I warn everyone who hears the words of the prophecy of this book: if anyone adds to them, God will add to him the plagues described in this book, and if anyone takes away from the words of the book of this prophecy, God will take away his share in the tree of life and in the holy city, which are described in this book. He who testifies to these things says, 'Surely I am coming soon.' Amen. Come, Lord Jesus! The grace of the Lord Jesus be with all. Amen."
-Revelation 22:18-21 (ESV)

Notes

ALSO BY MICHAEL FILIPEK

The Missing Key in Dispensational Eschatology

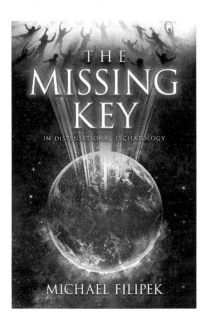

How is it that the Bible clearly describes the Rapture of the Church as an imminent, signless, and unpredictable event - yet also describes the beginning of the broad period of the Day of the Lord in this exact way? How can both of these end-time events truly be imminent? If one were to occur first, then logically, the other could not be described as "imminent." Similarly, how is it that the New Testament consistently portrays the rescue of the righteous as coinciding with the beginning of judgment for the wicked, with both being described as imminent?

Can it be that there is a simple biblical paradigm that, when consistently applied, easily clarifies these apparent dilemmas - one that most modern scholars have somehow overlooked? Can it harmonize all of the difficult and seemingly contradictory end-time Bible passages that have perplexed readers for generations? Join Michael Filipek as he carefully and meticulously pieces together this "missing key" paradigm in this comprehensive, first-of-its-kind study!

Available on Amazon in Kindle and paperback.

Made in the USA
Columbia, SC
06 September 2024

41919318R00070